THE
WATCH

TROIKA 20

THE

WATCH

AN APPRECIATION

AURUM PRESS

PAUL CLARK ◉ PHOTOGRAPHS BY GUY RYECART

First published in Great Britain 1998 by
Aurum Press Limited
25 Bedford Avenue
London WC1B 2AT

A catalogue record for this book is
available from the British Library

ISBN 1 85410 598 1

This book was conceived,
designed and produced by
THE IVY PRESS LIMITED
2/3 St Andrews Place
Lewes, East Sussex
BN7 1UP

Art Director: *Peter Bridgewater*
Editorial Director: *Sophie Collins*
Managing Editor: *Anne Townley*
Project Editor: *Caroline Earle*
Editor: *Julie Whitaker*
Designer: *Ron Bryant-Funnell*
Photography: *Guy Ryecart*

Printed and bound in China

Throughout this book the dimensions of
the watch faces are given in imperial and
metric measurements; height is expressed
by H, width is expressed by W, and
diameter is expressed by D.

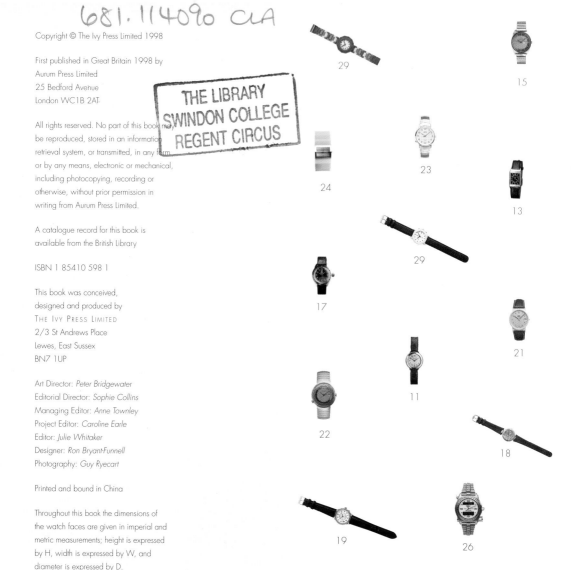

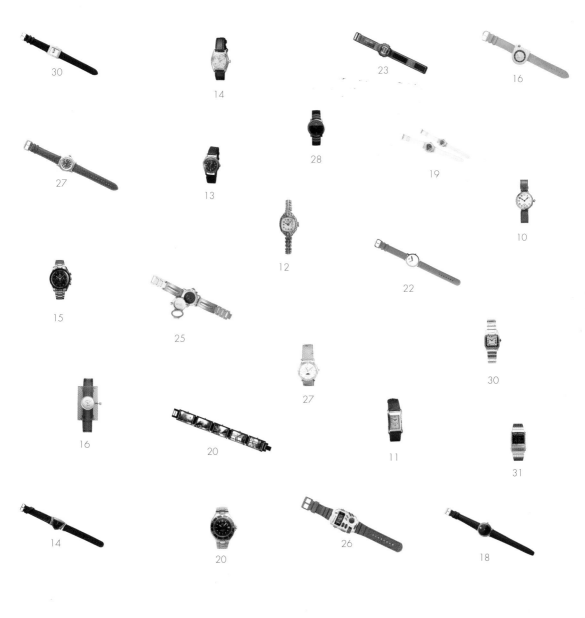

30

14

23

16

27

28

19

13

10

12

22

15

25

30

16

27

20

11

31

14

20

26

18

Introduction

One of the most prolifically manufactured complex objects in existence, the modern wristwatch is a marvel of technological achievement. Manufactured to withstand almost any environment, the watch is also a significant designer accessory – *and* it tells the time!

Half Hunter style wristwatch
1914

The wristwatch is a descendant of the pocket watch which, fashioned in precious metals with jewelled movements, was a traditional status symbol. The earliest wristwatches emerged in the late 19th century as an ornament on a lady's bracelet. Some of these were small converted pocket watches with side lugs added to fit a strap, with the winder at the top. The practicality of the wristwatch for men was soon realized, as it could easily be consulted without having to delve into a waistcoat pocket. During World War I, the wristwatch found favour with pilots and artillery officers, which helped to shed its reputation of effeminacy.

Early German
wristwatch
c1918

The European watch industry switched to wristwatch production, and it worked to high standards of excellence in time-keeping, quality and design to compete with the USA's mass-production methods. New products of the Machine Age began to influence watch design; for example, the Cartier 'Tank' watch was inspired by the rugged new weapon that had helped the Allies win World War I. Innovators such as Rolex, with their waterproof watches, entered the market.

Tank Français
Cartier, 1996

'Character' watches emerged from the gloom of the 1930s Depression years, aimed at the previously untapped juvenile market. The American Ingersoll company, which had pioneered the dollar pocket watch (selling 15 million between 1892 and 1906), shrewdly picked Mickey Mouse for their first wristwatches in 1933 – and he is still ticking along today.

The military requirements for functional watches during World War II created the 'instrument panel' style that is still popular today, and new demands of precise time-keeping in sports (particularly flying) led to a style of watch dial with separate second and part-of-second timer dials, which

Mickey Mouse watch
Bradley, 1970

became known as the chronograph.

Despite the rapid wartime technological advances in electronics, the mechanical (i.e. clockwork) movement was at the heart of all watches until the development of miniature electrical mechanisms in the 1950s. The first electric wristwatches were produced in the USA in 1957, made possible by the miniaturization of switches and batteries. New standards of time-keeping were realized with Bulova's electronic 'Acutron' in 1959, guaranteed to stay accurate to within a minute a month.

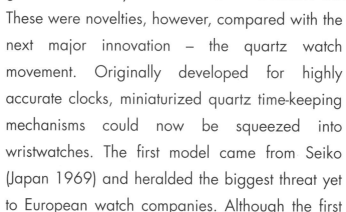

These were novelties, however, compared with the next major innovation – the quartz watch movement. Originally developed for highly accurate clocks, miniaturized quartz time-keeping mechanisms could now be squeezed into wristwatches. The first model came from Seiko (Japan 1969) and heralded the biggest threat yet to European watch companies. Although the first

Black watch
Sinclair, 1972

Calculator watch
Casio, c1980

quartz watches were expensive, costing up to $600 in 1970, prices tumbled when digital displays replaced traditional hour-and-minute hands. The world's first digital wristwatch using LEDs (light emitting diodes), was the 'Pulsar' produced in the US by the Hamilton Company in 1971. It was followed by the British Sinclair 'Black Watch' in 1972, but both suffered from short battery life. The arrival of the low-power-consuming Liquid Crystal Display (LCD) solved this problem.

In the 1970s and 1980s, plastic cases and electronic innards took over, and the upstart semiconductor industry swept away centuries of traditional methods. As circuitry became more complex, new features could be incorporated, as in Casio's calculator watch of 1978. Eventually there was a revival of the traditional hour-and-minute hand display, now combined with quartz accuracy. In 1983 the Swiss watch industry claimed another advance with the 'Swatch' watch. By incorporating streetwise style with state-of-the-art technology, the desirable disposable watch was created.

Warhol Times/5
Movado, 1988

Now, fashion trends demand reasonably-priced, sports-related designer watches. New and established fashion labels have launched countless designs, with a myriad of functions, all competing for a place on your wrist. By contrast, traditional watchmakers have turned to limited editions of very special watches, such as Andy Warhol's 'Times 5' design for Movado produced in an edition of 250, catering for the serious watch collector and connoisseur.

Wise Hand
Swatch, 1996

EARLY WRISTWATCH

One of the earliest forms of the wristwatch, which owed its design entirely to the pocket watch, but converted and scaled down, became easily accessible on the wearer's wrist. As other new inventions, such as the motor car, made life more complicated the practicality of the wristwatch became ever more clear.

GOLD-PLATED ALLOY CASE, 1928, D1.1IN / 2.7CM

GOLD AND WHITE GOLD CASE, 1929, H1.7IN X W1.4IN / H4.3CM X W3.5CM

HARWOOD SELF-WINDING

J. HARWOOD

The outstanding British watchmaker John Harwood perfected the self-winding watch in 1927. Although he obtained a patent and made prototypes of his watch, he was unable to find a British maker interested in manufacturing his revolutionary design. However, several innovative Swiss companies took up the rights and it was first manufactured by Blancpain in 1929.

ROLEX PRINCE

ROLEX/HANS WILSDORF

One of Humphrey Bogart's favourite watches, the Prince is a masterpiece of timeless design. The rectangular case that emerged after World War I marked a complete visual break from the style of the pocket watch. The Prince's design is still emulated in the 1990s, combining modernity with classicism.

INGERSOLL 'COCKTAIL'

INGERSOLL

Ingersoll established a reputation on both sides of the Atlantic for inexpensive watches for men and women. The advent of semi-professional positions for women (such as telephonists and secretaries) in the job market created a new class of consumer. The innovation of mass production made elegant ladies' watches, such as this inexpensive cocktail watch, readily available to this market.

REVERSO
JAEGER LE COULTRE

Jaeger le Coultre, renowned clock and watchmakers since 1833, created this watch for the 'sporting gentleman' in 1931. The watch case swivels through 180 degrees, and the back can be engraved with your personal crest should you possess one. Its stark, geometric simplicity makes it a masterpiece of modernism.

MILITARY WATCH
INTERNATIONAL WATCH COMPANY

The requirements of wartime conditions created a new aesthetic in watch design – the need to be both highly reliable and rugged. Matt black face, water resistant, together with luminous hands and quarter hours, this spartan style was to become a classic form for the real 'action man' of future generations.

GOLD OYSTER PERPETUAL

ROLEX/HANS WILSDORF

Hans Wilsdorf had created the waterproof Rolex in 1926, but was not satisfied with his brilliant innovation until it was also self-winding. He then set about perfecting a novel mechanism, launching the 'Perpetual' in 1931. These innovations, together with the watch's quality, reliability and craftsmanship, ensured the reputation of this enduring classic watch.

HAMILTON ELECTRIC 500

HAMILTON/ RICHARD ARBIB

As the possibility of a non-mechanical watch became feasible, many manufacturers attempted to perfect a battery-powered watch. Hamilton, the traditional US watchmakers famous for the 19th-century Railroad watch, beat the competition with this stunningly original asymmetric design. It is now being reproduced after once more achieving fame as an essential accessory in the hit film *Men in Black*.

STEEL AND GOLD-PLATED

CASE, 1940s,

D1.1IN / 2.9CM

PLATED STEEL CASE, 1957, H1.7 X W1.2IN / H4.4 X W3CM

**STAINLESS STEEL
CASE, 1965,**
D1.6IN / 4CM

**PLATED STEEL
CASE, 1959,**
D1.3IN / 3.2CM

ACUTRON
BULOVA/MAX HERTZEL

Devised in Switzerland but made in the USA, the Bulova Acutron was the first watch to incorporate a transistorized circuit. The humming Acutron, with its 'tuning fork' heart vibrating, startled the traditional watch industry with its incredible new standard of time-keeping, guaranteed to be accurate to within a minute a month.

SPEEDMASTER/ MOON WATCH
OMEGA/CLAUDE BAILLOD

Omega was one of the earliest brand names to be associated with high-performance, quality wristwatches. When NASA needed a reliable watch for its astronauts to wear in space, it tested several top brand names to destruction. The outstanding performance of the Omega model meant that this was the watch to go where no watch had ever gone before – the trusty and rugged Speedmaster adorned astronaut Neil Armstrong's wrist when he became the first man on the Moon in 1969. This is a commemorative version of Armstrong's watch, which had a special long strap to wear over his space suit. Like his, the watch has to be hand wound!

LIP MACH 2000
LIP COMPANY/ROGER TALLON

Although the Lip company had pioneered an electric watch in 1952, they subsequently suffered severe financial and labour problems. In a daring break with the past, the company asked train designer Roger Tallon to come up with a fresh new concept to help get the company back on track. Illustrated here is a re-issued version of his 1972 design. Tallon's revolutionary watch was the first to embrace plastics as the predominant material and to make the strap an integral part of the design concept.

PLASTIC-COATED BRASS, 1972, H1.6 X W1.7IN / H4 X W4.2CM

ACRYLIC, 1970s, H1.6 X W0.8IN / H4 X W2CM

GUCCI
ACRYLIC WATCH
GUCCI/SYLVIA KATZ

The glamour and colour of 1970s fashion, teamed with the exciting possibilities of plastics, inspired stylish, new matching accessories. Although famed for its 'G' watch, this Gucci design shows that there were fashionable, disposable watches long before the Swatch.

CHROME-PLATED STEEL, 1980s, DIA 1.2IN / 3CM

SOVIET 'PARACHUTIST'
WOSTOK FACTORY

The no-nonsense style of this macho mechanical watch with its patriotic symbols was inspired by the rugged aesthetic of the Eastern bloc military machine – its oversized winder is for a gloved hand. The retro-novelty of Soviet products such as this enjoyed a fashion fad after the fall of the Berlin Wall.

MUSEUM WATCH

MOVADO/GEORGE HORWITT

American designer George Horwitt conceived his totally original watch in 1947, but could not find a company interested in manufacturing it. Finally in 1961, after it had become the first watch design to be selected by the Museum of Modern Art in New York, Movado (part of the North American Watch Corporation group) began to manufacture the design. It is now their flagship model around the world.

THE ROCK WATCH

TISSOT/THOMKE

Nothing to do with the Flintstones! Not satisfied with co-inventing the Swatch, Dr Thomke also created another classic concept – the Rock Watch. This watch features an intriguing combination of million-year-old stone with the latest quartz mechanism. By using a variety of non-precious rocks meant that no two of these watches were indentical.

JELLY WATCH

SWATCH/ THOMKE, MULLER AND MOCK

Reeling from the shock of the quartz revolution, the Swiss watch industry was completely revitalized in 1983 with the creation of Thomke, Muller and Mock. Their fresh new ideas – an analogue watch with only 51 parts (as opposed to 125) and new designs every six months – helped the company to become a world leader in designer watches. Intended to be ephemeral, their designs ironically soon became highly collectable.

PLASTIC CASE AND STRAP, 1985,
D1.3IN / 3.3CM D0.9IN / 2.4CM

STAINLESS STEEL

CASE, 1987,

D1.4IN / 3.6CM

LINDBERGH HOUR ANGLE

LONGINES/ CHARLES LINDBERGH

There cannot have been many watches designed on solo flights across the Atlantic, but this watch was conceived by Charles Lindbergh during his epic 1927 flight, no doubt inspired by the earlier Longines chronometer that was strapped to his leg. It has now been re-issued as a commemorative tribute to Lindbergh's achievement.

TIMES/5

MOVADO/
ANDY WARHOL

Andy Warhol was an avid watch collector and had been developing an original design for Movado since 1981. Inspired by a string of five watches he had found, he devised this bracelet watch with five of his photos of New York as faces. It was his last work of art before his death in 1987.

TITANIUM CARBIDE
COATED STAINLESS
STEEL CASE, 1988,
H8.9 X W0.9IN /
H22.8 X W2.4CM

SEAMASTER 200M PROFESSIONAL

OMEGA

Keen to measure competitiveness, Omega has been the official time-keeper for every Olympic Games since 1932. Aimed at the sportsman, both above and below water, this super-resistant and waterproof, automatic titanium Seamaster is the culmination of Omega's range of rugged masculine watches. The 'Seamaster' range was introduced in 1970 and was the chosen watch of Jacques Cousteau, diver extraordinaire.

STAINLESS STEEL
CASE, 1988,
D1.41IN / 3.5CM

STAINLESS STEEL CASE, 1990, H1.6 X W1.2IN / H4 X W3CM

BRAUN AW 20

BRAUN/DIETER LUBS

Since they established themselves as a design-led company in the 1960s, Braun have consistently produced renowned minimalist and functional designs in the Bauhaus tradition. Their watches couple painstaking attention to detail with timeless design.

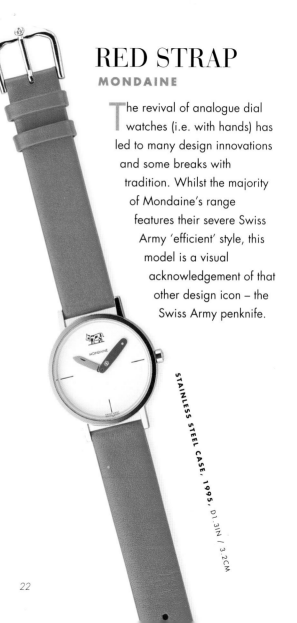

TITANIUM CASE, 1990, D1.6IN / 4CM

PORSCHE TRAVEL TIME

IWC/FERDINAND PORSCHE

Ferdinand Porsche, of car design fame, started his association with the International Watch Company in 1978 and has produced a series of impressive designs for them. This uncompromisingly practical titanium watch, in the best German design tradition, is for the international traveller, with a rotating bezel which indicates the time world-wide.

RED STRAP

MONDAINE

The revival of analogue dial watches (i.e. with hands) has led to many design innovations and some breaks with tradition. Whilst the majority of Mondaine's range features their severe Swiss Army 'efficient' style, this model is a visual acknowledgement of that other design icon – the Swiss Army penknife.

STAINLESS STEEL CASE, 1995, D1.3IN / 3.2CM

ZAMAC ALLOY CASE, 1990s, D1.3IN / 3.4CM

MERCURY INDIGLO

TIMEX/GILBERT MARQUIS

Timex is one of the largest watchmakers in the world (in 1960 it made eight million watches) with 2,000 models in its current range aimed at the mass market! The Mercury, designed in 1959, has now been brought up-to-date with the Indiglo system (patented by Timex in 1988), making it more versatile yet still retaining its classical good looks.

BABY-G-SHOCK

CASIO/ SEYMOUR POWELL

Baby-G is the 'soft' version of the famous 'G-shock' model. It resulted from the close collaboration between the British design team, Seymour Powell, and Casio, the world's largest manufacturer of digital watches. The macho qualities of its big brother have been deliberately minimized by the reduction of scale and the use of pastel colours.

POLYURETHANE PLASTIC, 1995, D1.7IN / 4.2CM

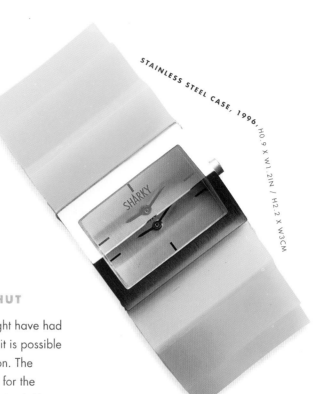

STAINLESS STEEL CASE, 1996, H0.9 X W1.2IN / H2.2 X W3CM

SHARKY

ALFEX/JANTJE FLEISCHHUT

Just as an earlier generation might have had a hat for every occasion, now it is possible to have a watch for every occasion. The Sharky is a striking fashion watch for the woman who really wants to be noticed. This watch is not for the shrinking violet – it screams pushy, bright and obvious. A chunky synthetic-rubber zig-zag bracelet, which comes in a variety of colours, complements its angular watch glass.

BRASS AND STEEL CASE, 1996, D1.7IN / 4.4CM

NEW ENFORCER
STORM/STEVE SUN

London-based Storm's watches are part of a range of exciting and original co-ordinated accessories aimed at the technophile consumer. The Enforcer, in chunky stainless steel, was designed by founder Steve Sun. His designs typically feature quirky details with a swivelling top lens compartment.

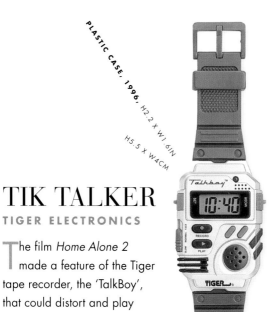

PLASTIC CASE, 1996, H2.2 X W1.6IN / H5.5 X W4CM

TITANIUM CASE, 1996, H2 X W1.8IN / H5 X W4.5CM

TIK TALKER

TIGER ELECTRONICS

The film *Home Alone 2* made a feature of the Tiger tape recorder, the 'TalkBoy', that could distort and play back a voice. Tiger, the company behind it, have produced this watch that looks like a film prop, it can do all the same things as the Talkboy and still tell the time!

EMERGENCY WATCH

BREITLING

Described as 'Sexy' hardware, the Breitling Emergency is the ultimate adventurer's watch. Developed in conjunction with NATO, it counts members of air forces around the world among its customers. To assist its intrepid wearers, the watch includes an emergency distress transmitter with a range of up to 250 miles (400 km) for those who find themselves marooned in some remote spot.

GOLD AND STEEL CASE, 1990s, D1.3IN / 3.3CM

ESPRIT 'SPORT FRESH'

ESPRIT

There is enormous competition in the high street for leading-edge, well-designed fashion watches. The Esprit range has borrowed from the rich history of watch design to offer a vibrant choice of watches suitable for outdoor pursuits – all are water resistant up to 150ft (50m).

BLANCPAIN MOON PHASE

BLANCPAIN

The aristocrats of watchmaking still regard the mechanical movement as the highest achievement of the watchmaker's craft and their skills are still respected by watch collectors and connoisseurs. Blancpain produce their hand-made masterpieces in a farmhouse workshop with a small team of craftsmen. This automatic perpetual calendar and moonphase is a classic of refined design.

STAINLESS STEEL CASE, 1996, D1.5IN / 3.8CM

MEGA SOLAR CERAMIC
JUNGHANS

The ultimate technological watch? Junghans have revolutionized clock and watch accuracy by linking them to ultra-precise radio transmissions. This watch's incredibly strong zirconium oxide case allows radio signals to pass through, which constantly adjust the time, even when the clocks change. Because it is powered by light, you don't have to worry about winding or batteries.

ZIRCONIUM OXIDE CERAMIC, 1990s, D1.6IN / 4CM

CHRONOMETER

TROIKA/ANDREW TSE

The style of the chronometer watch has survived the digital revolution, and its association with competitive activities – sports, racing and flying – continue to make it desirable. The traditional qualities of the classic dial have been re-interpreted by Andrew Tse in this very contemporary and affordable watch.

STAINLESS STEEL CASE, 1990s, D1.4IN / 3.7CM

LEGO® WATCH SYSTEM

LEGO/CHRISTOPHE WALCH

Having established their name in the playroom, LEGO are now invading the time-telling business. Tempting for the junior LEGO fan, or the postmodern adult, their 'build your own watch' system brings fun and games, and endless possibilities for your watch and strap combination.

POLYCARBONATE PLASTIC CASE, 1997, D1.6IN / 4CM

ALFEX 'ALTO'
ALFEX/TAKASHI KATO

Although the rectangular style of watch is deemed to be 'masculine', the Alto is one of a range of elegant designs intended as chic adornment for the young fashion-conscious woman. Its design is contemporary while drawing on the classic qualities of geometry and pleasing combinations of materials.

WHITE GOLD CASE, 1990s,
H1.6 X W1.1IN / H4 X W2.8CM

STAINLESS STEEL CASE, 1997,
H1.2 X W0.8IN / H3 X W2.1CM

SANTOS
CARTIER

Based on one of the earliest wristwatch designs by jeweller Louis Cartier for his friend, the aviator Alberto Santos Dumont, the Santos has become one of the most memorable and desirable watch designs. Its secret signature on the 'VII' is intended to reduce the likelihood of its being counterfeited – a fate that has befallen many of the famed watch marques.

FUTURIST

CASIO/MR KUBO

Casio have gone 'Back to the Future' with this ultra-high-tech-looking watch that incorporates Casio's 'Illuminator' technology. It shows that there is still life in the LCD concept, by raising its status from the anonymous black watch to this multifunction alarm chronograph that, as its name would suggest, looks as though it would make a suitable prop for the next science fiction blockbuster.

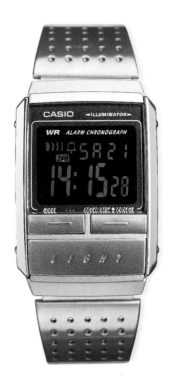

METALLIC FINISHED RESIN, 1997, H1.7I X W1.2IN / H4.2 X W3CM

ACKNOWLEDGEMENTS

The publishers would particularly like to
thank the following for loan of watches:

Artworks: 22 (right),29 (left)
Baume & Co: 19 (right)
**British Horological Museum,
Upton:** 6, 7 (left), 8 (right),10, 11 (left),
12 (left), 17
Cartier Ltd: 7 (left), 30 (right)
Casio Electronics Co Ltd: 8 (right),
23 (right), 31
Ieva Clark: 9 (left)
James Evans: 20
H.H.H. Ltd: 18 (left), 24, 30 (left)
Hamilton/S M H: 14 (right)
Inter-city (Swiss Time) Ltd: 27 (right)
Junghans UK Ltd: 28
Sylvia Katz: 16 (centre)
Austin Kaye: 1, 22 (left)
Lip France: 16 (left), 32
Chris and Carol McEwan: 19 (left)
Omega/S M H: 15 (right), 20 (right)
Sun 99 Ltd: 25
Tiger Electronics UK: 26 (left)
Time Developments Ltd: 29 (right)
TWG Distribution: 26 (right)
UK Time Ltd: 23 (left)

Special thanks: Michael Balfour,
Alyson Green, James Gurney, Jane McAfee,
Seymour Powell, Stephen Reece-Raybould,
Martin Tobler

**The publishers wish to thank the
following for the use of pictures:**

Courtesy of Sotheby's: 11 (right), 12
(right), 13, 14 (left)
Christie's Images: 27 (left)
Movado: 9, 20 (left)

Endpapers: Self-winding wristwatch
mechanism of John Harwood

The registered trademark **LEGO**® is used
with special permission of the LEGO Group

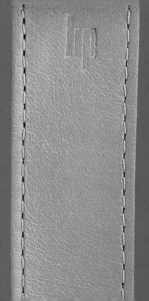